MW00513732

Simple Green Smoothies

Quick and healthy recipes

Author

Leonarda R. Hicks

COPYRIGHT

The author reserves all rights. Except for the use of a brief quotation in a book review, this book or any portion of it may not be reproduced or used in any way without the publisher's express written permission.

TABLE OF CONTENTS

Contents page

TABLE OF CONTENTS

1st Section

Introduction

Green smoothies are blended drinks made with leafy greens, fruits, vegetables, and healthy fats like almonds, hemp seeds, flax, and coconut. Spinach, kale, rainbow chard, mint, parsley, and collard greens are all popular leafy greens. Some people prefer to use only fresh, raw ingredients, while others claim that using frozen fruit gives the dish a thicker, ice cream-like texture.

Green smoothies are usually made up of the following ingredients:

Green vegetables should make up 40–50% of your diet (roughly half),

Usually raw green leafy vegetables like spinach, kale, swiss chard, collard greens, celery, parsley, or broccoli, with mostly or entirely fruit as the remaining ingredients. Wheatgrass and spirulina are two other health-promoting foods.

ingredients. When served raw, most green leafy vegetables have a bitter flavor, but this can be mitigated by using less bitter vegetables (such as baby spinach) or combining with fruit (e.g. banana softens both the flavor and texture). Some blender companies are now focusing their efforts on a specific demographic.

Green smoothies are encouraged to be made, and a recipe booklet is available.

The mixed juice doesn't even need to be blended like a smoothie if both the fruit and green vegetable ingredients are juiced ahead of time.

Green juice, for example.

When it comes to diabetes, smoothies can be beneficial.

Smoothies may appear to be high in sugar. While this is true for a lot of store-bought options, you have complete control at home. This is what prompted me to search for low-sugar, low-carbohydrate recipes.

Smoothies that are safe for diabetics

What's even better? These aren't just tasty snacks. They are low-calorie smoothie recipes that will aid in weight loss. You'll love how quick they are to prepare, especially on days when you're too busy or lazy to cook.

On other days, all you want is a cold drink to refresh you.

Fruits and vegetables contain nutrients.

Vegetables help to maintain a healthy balance of nutrients in the body.

At the same time, you'll be able to manage your glucose levels and your weight.

It is suggested that you use whole fruits and vegetables in your recipes.

Vegetable smoothies, rather than juices, are the healthier option.

Juices lack the fiber your body requires.

Smoothies with diabetic-friendly ingredients

It's important to remember that the ingredients you use in your smoothie will determine whether it's healthy or unhealthy.

Smoothies are a great way to get ingredients that help regulate blood sugar levels on a daily basis!

The American Diabetes Association has published a list of ten foods that all diabetics should consume in order to maintain their health.

Your diet will be boosted.

These foods have a low glycemic index (GI) and provide important nutrients like calcium, potassium, fiber, magnesium, and vitamins A (as carotenoids),

C, and E that aren't usually found in sufficient amounts in the typical western diet.

Do you have any friends or relatives who are expecting? Be sure to inform them.

regarding these smoothie recipes for pregnant women!

Here are the ones we think are best for diabetic smoothies among the superfoods recommended by the ADA:

Leafy Dark Green Vegetables (spinach, parsley, etc.)

Collards and kale (recipes here) – because they're low in calories and carbs, they're an excellent superfood to include in your smoothies.

Fruit Citrus (grapefruit, oranges, lemons)

– For a good dose of vitamin C, use freshly squeezed juice, or cut into cubes for soluble fiber. An appliance that combines a juicer and a blender would be useful in this situation. Here are some reviews of blender/food processor combos.

Sweet potatoes give your smoothies a creamy texture and sweetness, as well as vitamin A and fiber.

Berries – whichever variety you use, berries will add color and flavor to your smoothies while also providing antioxidants, vitamins, and fiber.

Healthy fats and magnesium can be found in nuts and seeds. To add creaminess to your smoothies, either use nut butters or grind flaxseed for an omega-3 fatty acid boost.

If you're not a vegetarian, fat-free milk and yogurt would be your smoothie's base liquid.

For diabetics, the best smoothies are

Smoothies may appear to be a healthy choice, and they can be a good way to get fiber and other nutrients from fruits and vegetables. However, the wrong type of smoothie, especially when eating out, can be a bad choice for people with diabetes.

Smoothies are a tasty way to eat more fruits and vegetables.

Superfoods like spinach and green leaves should be consumed. Other ingredients, on the other hand, may be high in fat and sugar, putting you at risk for blood sugar spikes and weight gain.

A diabetic can enjoy smoothies while minimizing the negative effects by following a few simple guidelines.

1. Eat a variety of fats that are good for you.

Avocado and chia seeds, for example, are both good sources of healthy fats that can be added to smoothies.

For diabetics, certain fats are beneficial. Fats are important in the body because they can help slow down the rate at which sugar enters the bloodstream and make a person feel satisfied.

Almond or peanut butter are two healthy fat sources to add to a morning smoothie.

seeds of chia

• avocado

• pecans in their natural form

Walnuts, raw

Too much fat, on the other hand, can lead to weight gain, so the quantities must be balanced.

2. Include protein in your recipe.

Protein, like fat, has a slew of health benefits that are important for everyone, but especially diabetics.

Protein-rich foods may help to slow down the aging process.

Sugar enters the bloodstream at a slower rate as a result of slower absorption of food.

Animal or vegetable proteins can be used.

based. Making a smoothie with high-protein ingredients can be beneficial to your health.

Proteins that work well in smoothies are:

• Greek yogurt that is plain and unsweetened

• seeds, including hemp and others

• almonds

• protein derived from pea

• protein made from whey

• milk with reduced fat

3. Get your fiber fix.

Adding leafy greens, such as spinach, to a smoothie can make it more nutritious and fiber-rich.

Soluble and insoluble fibers are two types of fiber.

Soluble fiber is more difficult to digest by the body. This means it takes longer for its energy to be released, lowering the risk of a glucose spike.

Insoluble fiber improves digestive health and reduces food absorption in the gastrointestinal tract.

Fiber can make you feel fuller for longer periods of time.

These factors can help a diabetic person by lowering the risk of: blood sugar spikes

cholesterol build-up

Overeating due to a lack of fullness results in weight gain.

Fiber can help people with diabetes and high blood sugar avoid complications and improve their overall health in these ways.

Most fruits, such as raspberries, oranges, nectarines, peaches, and blueberries, as well as leafy greens like spinach and kale, and nuts, are high-fiber foods that might work well in a smoothie.

Seeds of chia

4. Don't use sugar to flavor

Sugar is present in many foods, and some contain sugar that is hidden.

Processed

Sugar is frequently added to ready-to-eat foods.

Remember the following when choosing ingredients:

Sugary syrups are used to keep some canned fruits fresh.

Sugar comes in the form of honey and maple syrup.

Milk contains lactose, which is also a sugar. Ripe fruits have more sugar than less ripe fruits.

Sugar may be present in almond, soy, and other milk substitutes.

In moderation, these might be okay. Spices like cinnamon, nutmeg, ginger, or turmeric fruit, which has a natural source of sugar, as well as fiber nuts, are other ways to add flavor.

The addition of oats can give a creamy texture to a dish.

In moderation, use dates and dried fruit

unsweetened cocoa powder fresh herbs such as mint, basil, or coriander

vanilla, almond, peppermint, or other extracts, but not syrups coffee, black

peanut butter in its original state

Because researchers still don't know exactly how sweeteners might affect a

person with diabetes, it's best to sweeten smoothies with natural ingredients

instead of adding sweeteners.

5. Eat 3 carbohydrate servings

When creating a smoothie, a diabetic should keep track of how many carbs

are in it.

In general, diabetics should aim for a smoothie that has 45 grams (g) or fewer carbs. At least three distinct carbohydrate kinds should be included.

15g servings of a variety of foods

People often add the following carbs to smoothies:

a banana, tiny melon, 1 cup

blueberries, 3/4 cup plain yogurt, 1 cup

granola (12 cup)

Greens, spinach, or other dark leafy vegetables may be added to the smoothie to make it more nutritious. These have less carbohydrates per serving and are good for you.

It's easy to estimate how many carbs to add in the smoothie by using measuring cups, spoons, and the diabetic exchange list.

A doctor can tell you how many carbohydrates you should eat each day and at what times.

each meal – this may vary depending on what you're eating.

Individuals are classified according to their height, weight, amount of exercise, and medicines.

6. Turn it into a dinner.

Although a smoothie may seem to be a drink, it may contain as many carbohydrates and calories as a complete meal.

Take into account the smoothie's carb and calorie content and use it as a meal replacement or a light snack.

If a full breakfast or lunch is still appealing, go for a lighter option.

As a beverage, choose sparkling water, unsweetened tea, or coffee.

Fruits and vegetables with a low glycemic index (GI).

Smoothies made from vegetables are an excellent choice. The glycemic index (GI) is a metric that determines how rapidly a meal raises blood sugar levels.

A lower GI indicates that the sugar will be absorbed more slowly by the body than a higher GI item. Low GI meals are less likely to trigger blood sugar spikes as a result of this.

Water has the lowest GI of 0 while glucose has the highest GI of 103.

Because they contain varied levels of sugar and fiber, all fruits and vegetables have different GI ratings.

Here are some examples of items that might be used in a smoothie, along with their GI ratings:

Foods that have a low GI (55 or less) oranges\sbanana

dates

cooked carrots with plain yogurt

rolled oats porridge

soy milk and other kinds of milk Foods with a GI of 56–69 are those with a medium glycemic index (GI

cooked sweet potato, pumpkin, pineapple

Foods that have a high GI (70 and above) oat porridge made in a flash rice with watermelon

However, just because something has a low GI score doesn't imply you may put as much of it in a smoothie as you like.

When creating smoothies, keep in mind that even if a fruit has a low GI, the carbohydrate content must still be taken into consideration.

As a fruit ripens, its GI score climbs.

Juicing, mixing, and cooking boost the score. Because the sugar in orange juice is absorbed more rapidly by the body, it has a higher GI than a whole orange.

8. Increase the volume of the dish

Although a smoothie may seem to be a meal, it is really a meal substitute.

Smoothies should be consumed in moderation if a person still need a meal to feel satisfied.

According to one source, a daily smoothie of 150 milliliters (ml) is plenty.

The following are some more options:

adding ice mass adding water to dilute the solid components

9. Suggestions for smoothie ordering

When ordering a smoothie outside of the house, inquire about the ingredients and check if the service can produce one without added sugar. It is better to pick another drink if they are unable to do so.

Some establishments prepare smoothies as customers wait, allowing them to choose precise ingredients.

10. Additional factors to think about

High blood pressure, obesity, celiac disease, and lactose intolerance are some of the symptoms and problems that people with diabetes may face.

Other factors might restrict your options.

There are many different ingredients that may be used to make a smoothie.

Lactose intolerance is a condition in which someone is unable to consume lacto

For those who choose not to consume dairy, unsweetened almond or soy milk is an acceptable substitute.

Lactose intolerant people should avoid adding dairy milk or dairy milk byproducts like yogurt to their smoothies.

Almond or soy milk are also excellent options.

In most smoothie recipes, they may be used for dairy milk.

Because certain milk replacements are rich in sugar, people should pick unsweetened milk alternatives or verify the sugar level of a product before buying and consuming it.

Celiac disease is a condition that affects people who have gluten

Celiac disease is more common in type 1 diabetes patients than in the general population, according to research.

Gluten, a protein found in wheat, rye, and barley, must be avoided by celiac disease sufferers.

Depending on the brand, whey protein can contain gluten.

Although whey is gluten-free in and of itself, there are some products that contain gluten.

Gluten fillers are added to products by manufacturers.

Before purchasing whey products or experimenting with other plant-based proteins, always read the label.

Obesity

Those who are overweight or obese must keep a close eye on their calorie intake.

It may be beneficial to emphasize plant foods and fiber.

In general, a smoothie that is good for diabetics is also good for weight loss.

High blood pressure and cholesterol levels are two of the most common health problems today.

High-fiber, low-fat foods, such as beets, nuts, and seeds, and green leaves, are recommended for people with high blood pressure and cholesterol.

fruits

milk with less fat

Foods containing added salt should be avoided by people with high blood pressure.

Smoothie Health Benefits

Smoothies can be a complete meal, with enough protein, carbohydrates, fiber, and fat to satisfy a person for several hours.

Fruit smoothies

Vitamins, minerals, and other nutrients can be found in foods like vegetables, nuts, and seeds. All

A person's overall health can benefit from these nutrients.

Proper nutrition can help a person lower their cholesterol, lose weight, gain muscle, improve their nervous and circulatory systems, and increase their energy levels.

Risks

When ordering or making a smoothie, keep in mind that, despite its appearance, a smoothie can contain as many carbs and calories as a meal. Food should not be consumed.

a complete meal and a fruit smoothie

Furthermore, while smoothie ingredients may contain fiber, blending food breaks down fiber, making it easier for the body to digest.

When a person consumes fruits, vegetables, and other high-fiber foods in a smoothie rather than eating them whole and unprocessed, they will be less satisfying and more likely to cause a blood sugar spike.

People should not get all of their fruits and vegetables from smoothies; instead, they should get the majority of their nutrients from whole foods.

Takeaway

A smoothie is a healthy and delicious way to start the day or to get a fruit or vegetable snack in between meals.

A diabetic should, however, check the ingredients to ensure there is no added sugar.

To ensure that smoothies contain healthy ingredients, it is best to make them at home.

People with diabetes should avoid fruit-only smoothies and keep track of how much carbohydrate they consume in each smoothie, as this has a direct impact on blood sugar levels.

Smoothies with fruits, a healthy fat like peanut butter, chia seeds, or coconut oil, and a healthy protein like hemp seed or Greek yogurt can help balance the smoothie and prevent blood sugar spikes.

Smoothies with a lot of sugar can be dangerous.

When consuming smoothies, people should keep this in mind. Also, because smoothies are a liquid, don't eat too much of them.

Whole foods are more filling than liquids and can help you avoid overeating by making you feel satisfied sooner.

Foods that don't cause a spike in blood sugar

Garlic Avocados

Cherries with a tart flavor Veggies with Vinegar Chia seeds are a type of seed that comes from the Whole grains Cacao berries Nuts Eggs

Coffee

Takeaway

To reverse prediabetes, you must eat a healthy diet. Blood sugar can't be lowered with foods, herbs, drinks, or supplements. Medication and physical activity are the only things that can help.

However, there are foods and beverages with a low Glycemic Index that you can eat and drink (GI).

This means that these foods won't cause a blood sugar spike and may even help you avoid one. Staying or becoming active, in addition to dietary changes, is essential.

Avocados

Avocados are high in good fats and may help to prevent metabolic syndrome.

Polyunsaturated fatty acids (PUFAs) and monounsaturated fatty acids (MUFAs) are essential components of a blood sugar-controlling diet. Insulin sensitivity can be improved by them. They can also help with satiety and blood pressure, as well as inflammation. Avocados contain a lot of MUFAs.

Avocados have been shown in studies to lower metabolic syndrome risk. This is a group of risk factors that can raise your chances of developing diabetes. It can also increase the risk of blood vessel disease, such as heart attack and stroke.

Avocados have a low glycemic index (GI) as well. Make Oh She Glow's raw avocado chocolate pudding, which has no added sugar, for a unique, diabetes-friendly dessert.

Omega-3-rich fish such as tuna, halibut, and salmon

Protein aids in the maintenance and repair of the human body.

self-correction Protein has no effect on your body.

It has no GI rating and will not cause blood sugar levels to rise. Protein also increases satiety, so eating it instead of bread, rice, or pasta to feel full could be a good way to keep your blood sugar under control.

Protein is abundant in fish. It contains a good amount of omega-3 fatty acids and is low in unhealthy fats. Salmon trout albacore tuna are some good choices.

halibut (mackerel)

Fish can also be prepared quickly and easily. Preheat the oven to 425°F (218°C) and season a filet with salt, pepper, and lemon. Preheat the oven to 200°F and bake for 20 minutes, or until the meat is flaky.

Garlic

Garlic has the potential to aid blood sugar management. Garlic consumption has been shown to lower fasting blood glucose levels, which is the level of blood sugar when you haven't eaten. According to similar research, Onions have blood sugar-lowering properties.

Garlic has no GI because it contains no carbohydrates and therefore does not raise blood sugar levels. Try this delicious garlic spread from An Edible Mosaic to add more garlic to your meals. It can be used instead of butter or salad dressing for up to a week.

Cherries with a tart flavor

While all fruits have the potential to raise blood sugar levels, some, such as sour cherries, have a lower GI. Anthocyanins, a pigment found in sour cherries, are a type of pigment. Studies

Anthocyanins may protect against diabetes and obesity, according to new research.

Instead of bananas, pears, and apples, eat more sour cherries if you like fruits.

Instead of peach cobbler, try I Breathe, I'm Hungry's paleo cherry crisp with no added sugar. Because regular cherries have a moderate to high GI score, make sure you use sour cherries.

Vinegar of the apple

Apple cider vinegar's acetic acid

In the stomach, it lowers the activity of certain enzymes.

According to one study, apple cider is good for your health.

Following a meal, vinegar can help you feel more insulin sensitive.

20 g of apple cider is a good starting point.

To avoid a blood sugar spike, mix 40 grams of vinegar with 40 grams of water before eating.

Spinach, kale, and chard are leafy greens.

Kale is nutrient-dense and versatile, and can be used in a variety of dishes.

Fiber is abundant in leafy greens.

Magnesium and vitamin A are two of these nutrients. These nutrients may assist in the reduction of blood pressure.

sugar. To include in your diet, leafy greens such as:

lettuce-spinach collards

greens of turnip kale

chard de Suisse

Instead of 1,35 servings, you should eat 1.35 servings.

A daily intake of two servings of leafy greens is linked to a 14 percent lower risk of type 2 diabetes.

Low GI foods include all leafy greens. Spinach has a GI of under one per one cup. Kale has a GI score that ranges from 2 to 4 on a scale of 1 to 10. Try this diabetic-friendly smoothie from Tracy Russell of Incredible Smoothies to get more leafy greens in your diet. Chia seeds are a type of seed that comes from the

Chia seeds are high in fiber, healthy fats, omega-3s, calcium, and antioxidants, and are a good source of these nutrients. High-chia seed diets have been shown to lower LDL cholesterol and triglycerides in studies.

Chia seeds have a GI of 1 and are a delicious addition to any recipe. In this Little Broken Pudding recipe, the gooey texture works well as a thickener (skip the maple syrup). Nutrition To make a low-carb pizza crust, Stripped uses chia seeds and cauliflower. Cacao

Chocolatey spreads and treats such as cocoa butter and chocolate are made with cacao. It's bitter and unsweetened like dark chocolate before confectioners add sugar.

The antioxidant content of cacao seeds is high. They also contain epicatechin, a flavanol that activates key proteins to regulate glucose production. Even in those with diabetes, it can help to keep blood sugar levels in check.

Substitute dark chocolate with at least 70% cacao content for the milk chocolate. Cacao nibs can also be added to yogurt, smoothies, and desserts as a garnish.

Blackberries and blueberries are two different kinds of berries.

Blackberries and blueberries aren't as high in sugar as other fruits.

fruits. These berries have the highest concentrations of anthocyanins and are high in fiber. Certain digestive enzymes are inhibited by anthocyanins, which causes digestion to be slowed. They also keep blood sugar levels from rising after starch-heavy meals.

According to one study, including blueberry bioactive (22.5 g) in smoothies improved insulin sensitivity in people who were insulin resistant.

Blueberries have a 5 glycemic index. The blueberry peach chia seed parfait will satisfy your sweet tooth.

Other nuts, such as almonds

Although almonds have the lowest GI score, they aren't the only nuts that can help manage blood sugar levels.

Almonds can help prevent diabetes by helping to regulate and reduce blood sugar spikes after meals. Fasting glucose and insulin levels were found to be lower in people who consumed 2 ounces of almondsTrusted Source per day in one study. In another study, people with prediabetes who ate almonds had higher insulin sensitivity.

Almonds have a GI of 0 according to the USDA. This is due to the fact that fiber makes up the majority of the carbohydrate in almonds and other nuts. EatingWell's Chinese chicken noodle salad, or toasted almonds with cumin to make a healthy snack. Try kelp (seaweed) or shirataki (yam) noodles in the noodle salad for a low-carb alternative.

The GI scores of most nuts are low, ranging from 0 to 20. The nut that has a higher score is the winner.

The cashew GI score (22). Instead of crackers and other snacks, reach for nuts like pistachios, walnuts, and macadamias the next time you're hungry.

Grain, whole

Whole grains (such as millet or quinoa) should be preferred over "white grains" when shopping or dining out. Grain is white.

are high in carbs and can cause blood sugar to spike. Whole grains contain more fiber, phytochemicals, and nutrients, which can aid in blood sugar regulation.

Whole grain was discovered to be beneficial in one study.

Insulin sensitivity was improved by eating. After eating, fasting insulin levels dropped by 10%. The GI score for whole-grain bread is 51, and the GI score for whole-grain pasta is 42.

Eggs

Eggs have a bad reputation as a high-cholesterol food. Those with prediabetes, on the other hand, appear to be unaffected by egg consumption. Dietary cholesterol is also thought to be less important.

Those without type 2 diabetes, at the very least.

Eggs have a GI of 0 like all other pure protein sources. Eggs can also help you feel more satisfied and less hungry. However, what you put in your eggs can negate their nutritional value. Hardboiled eggs can be a satisfying snack or quick breakfast if consumed in moderation.

Coffee

According to research, drinking one cup of coffee per day (both caffeinated and decaffeinated) can help you lose weight.

may reduce your chances of developing type 2 diabetes by more than 10%. But it's also important what you put in your coffee. Sugar, syrups, and milk should not be added to your coffee in excess.

Finally,

Avoid foods with a high GI score if you want to prevent diabetes and prediabetes through diet. Reduce your sugar and total carbohydrate intake as well. Foods with a GI of 55 or less are considered low-GI.

There are a number of apps that help you find healthier eating options. These apps can be used to check the weather forecast.

food sugar and carbohydrate content You can avoid sugar and carbohydrate spikes by doing so. Among these are:

If you're insulin resistant, losing weight, exercising, and eating a balanced, whole foods diet are the most important things you can do to avoid diabetes. There is no single method, food, or workout that can replace the long-term advantages of a balanced diet.

The three most significant advantages of going green are as follows:

Type 2 diabetes smoothies include the following:

1 – Weight Loss: Being overweight is a well-known risk factor for developing type 2 diabetes.

Those who lose weight through diet and exercise are more likely to have their diabetes reversed and managed effectively. Green smoothies are a great way to increase your fruit and vegetable intake while also losing weight.

2 – Exercise Energy: Exercising is a great way to boost your energy levels.

another technique for reducing diabetes symptoms and severity. The vast majority of the people I've met have been extremely helpful.

Green smoothie drinkers who were polled said they had more energy and exercised more. Green smoothies are a great source of vitamins and minerals.

3 – Improved Nutrition Green overall.

Smoothies are the first step toward a diet and lifestyle change. The vast majority of people who drink green smoothies on a regular basis eat far fewer processed foods, according to the people I've interviewed. Their diet shifts toward a plant-based, low-calorie, high-nutrient, health-promoting diet.

SECOND PART

The Perfect Breakfast

Smoothie Recipe for Diabetics

Breakfast options abound. Almonds and cocoa smoothie is a great option.

This recipe is ideal because it is, first and foremost, delicious. Second, cocoa

is well-known for its cholesterol-lowering properties, making it an excellent

choice for weight loss. If you have type 2 diabetes, cocoa lowers your insulin

resistance, allowing your blood sugar to stay under control. It is possible to

extract.

Buy unsweetened almond milk or make your own almond milk, which is my

preferred method.

Green tea powder, when combined with the other ingredients, forms a superfood.

Ingredients

Almond milk, 1 cup

1 tbsp. cocoa powder (unsweetened) green tea, 1 tablespoon

a pound of raspberries (frozen)

Instructions

Blend all of the ingredients together until smooth, then sip on this decadent chocolate beverage.

Smoothie recipe for diabetic lunch

The simplicity of this recipe is what appeals to me the most.

There is no need for a sweetener because it is so delicious. For the whole family, it's a huge hit. The flavors of apple and carrot effectively mask the taste of spinach. It's perfect for lunch due to its thick, creamy texture. It will assist you in avoiding the need to eat snacks prior to dinner.

Ingredients

12 peeled and cored apple 1 carrot (1 medium)

spinach, 1 cup

12 c. unsweetened almond milk

12 cubes of ice Instructions

To make the sauce, combine all of the ingredients in a blender and process until smooth and creamy.

Smoothie for diabetic dinner

If you're looking for a simple, easy-to-digest recipe to help you get through the day.

My father has a habit of waking up in the middle of the night.

Glucose levels are skyrocketing, and there's nothing you can do about it.

because he ate too much and his stomach couldn't handle it This non-dairy, light, and refreshing smoothie can be served as a dessert or as a meal replacement.

Ingredients

12 c. raspberries, frozen kale (cup)

1 gallon of soymilk 6 cubes ice

Instructions

To make the sauce, combine all of the ingredients in a blender and process until smooth.

Yogurt-based diabetic smoothie The muesli gives the mixture a unique flavor. It's worth noting that the yogurt is low in fat. You could substitute a fresh pear for the apple in the smoothie.

Servings: 1 glass of juice Ingredients

1 peeled, cored, and finely chopped apple muesli, 2 tblsp

Low-fat yogurt carton, 150 g

cold skimmed milk, 150 mL (1/4 pint) Instructions

In a food processor or blender, combine all of the ingredients and process until smooth.

Quickly serve.

Almond milk-based diabetic smoothie

If you don't want a sweet smoothie, this savory version made with unsweetened almond milk is a great alternative.

Yes, avocado, cherries, and berries go well together.

1 smoothie per person Ingredients

1 cup dark sweet or sour cherries, pitted and frozen

12 CUP UNSWEETENED BLUEBBER (FRESH OR FROZEN)

avocado (12 pound)

1 quart unsweetened almond milk (optional: vanilla-flavored)

Instructions

To make the sauce, combine all of the ingredients in a blender and process until smooth.

Strawberry juice for diabetics The diabetic strawberry smoothie is depicted in a glass with two straws and a strawberry.

It was simple to choose a strawberry smoothie. They're sugar-free, and the color of the smoothie is stunning. I prefer sweetener-free recipes. The sugar content is kept to a bare minimum as a result of this. Ingredients

12 cup strawberries (frozen) collard greens, 1 cup

12 c. soy milk, unsweetened

Instructions

In a blender, mix together all of the ingredients.

Blend until the consistency you want is reached.

Cool and serve.

Recipe for a chocolate and peanut butter smoothie for gestational diabetes.

One of my closest friends, who is expecting a child, gave me the idea for this dish. This recipe was chosen because you liked it.

You're welcome to have it on one of your days off.

I'm depressed. Ice cream or chocolate would be ideal, but they contain a lot of sugar, which will cause your blood sugar to spike. This one provides natural sweetness while remaining a safe choice. You'll be enamored with how the ingredients combine to make a delectable smoothie that also looks fantastic. The berries add a touch of color and flavor. To make it diabetic friendly, I decided to make a few changes.

Ingredients

water (12 cup)

12 c. soy or almond milk, unsweetened 1 tablespoon peanut butter (natural)

1 tbsp. cocoa powder (unsweetened) a handful of your preferred frozen

berries Instructions

A blender is used to combine all of the ingredients. Until the mixture is

smooth and creamy.

Smoothie recipe with peaches for diabetics Fresh peaches and frozen peaches

are both available. Both of these smoothies are delicious and nutritious. The

best part is that no additional sweetener is required.

1 smoothie per person 12 cup skim milk Ingredients

1 can (15 oz.) drained peach slices (or 1 cup sliced fresh peaches)

14 cup nonfat peach yogurt with artificial sweetener

Sweetener produced artificially (optional) ice cubes (cup)

Instructions

In a blender, combine the milk, peaches, and yogurt and process until smooth.

Taste and adjust the artificial sweetener as needed.

Blend in pulses on high until smooth after each addition of ice cubes.

Right away, serve.

Leftovers can be frozen in a microwave-safe container and thawed in 10-second increments until slushy in the microwave.

Smoothie with Kiwi for Diabetics

When kiwis are in season, savor them for their unique flavor.

They're one of the few fruits that have a creamy texture.

Because kiwis aid in digestion, this recipe makes a thick smoothie that's perfect for dinner.

Servings: There are four components.

3 peeled and sliced kiwifruit

2 frozen medium bananas, cut into 4 pieces

1 cup plain yogurt (fat-free) 14 tsp almond extract 3 tbsp honey (optional)

12 CUP ICE, CRUMBLED Instructions

In a blender, blend together the kiwi, banana, honey, yogurt, and almond extract. For at least 15 minutes, or until a smooth puree forms, blend on high speed.

Blend in the ice until the mixture is smooth and well combined.

Fill tall glasses with ice and serve. Right away, serve.

Green smoothie recipe for diabetics.

Most likely, you've experimented with a number of different things.

By now, you've probably had enough of green smoothies.

They're a superb option.

I've made this the best green smoothie for diabetics by making a few changes. It's low in carbohydrates and high in nutrients. The mint leaves give this Greek yogurt-based smoothie an unexpected twist of flavor. Ingredients

water (12 cup)

1 cup yogurt, greek

kale (cup)

1 tsp. protein powder

Mint leaves (a handful) Instructions

Combine all of the ingredients in a blender and chill until ready to serve.

Enjoy.

Smoothie with berries in season

On a busy morning, this is a great breakfast.

1 portion

5 minute preparation

Ingredients

50g raspberries in the freezer 50g strawberry (frozen) sugar-free and calorie-free sweetener, 200ml skimmed milk, to taste

1 tbsp low-fat live yogurt, 1 tbsp sour cream, 1 tbsp sour cream, 1 tbsp sour

Adding probiotics to your diet is a great way to improve your overall health.

Other fruits like mango, banana, peaches, nectarines, or just one type of berry could be used instead. You should not need to add sweetener if you use very ripe fruits.

✓

Summerberries have fewer carbs than tropical fruits like bananas and mangoes.

Substitute tofu for dairy.

plant-based milk, unsweetened and fortified

Diabetic Green Smoothie Recipes

1 banana

Blueberries, a handful

2 tsp. chia seeds, soaked kale (cup)

spinach, 1 cup Recipe of Allan An orange of considerable size kale (cup)

spinach (2 cups)

celery, 3 stalks

6-8 ounces Minute Maid brand light lemonade a medium or large cucumber 5 ice cubes

Recipe of Cara

a banana, frozen

greens, 1-2 cup (I rotate between chard, collard greens, spinach and kale)

1 cup frozen or fresh fruit (I alternate between berries, pineapple, pomegranate seeds/arils, mango, grapes, and other fruits)

1–2 tablespoons flax or chia seed, ground

1–2 tsp cinnamon

ginger root, 1/2 inch segment

Trisha's Recipe is a quick and easy way to make a delicious meal

4 cups kale, spinach, chard, collards, etc (spinach, kale, cabbage, beet greens, etc.)

chia seeds (about 2 tbsp) (soaked) flax seeds, 2 tblsp

celery, two stalks

cucumbers, 2 small

ginger root, 1 inch

a pear or an apple blueberries, half a cup pineapple (quarter cup)

Combine ice and water in a blender and process until smooth.

Lana's Green Smoothie is a refreshing green smoothie made with kale, spinach, and

Spinach (handful)

cucumber (three slices) celery half-stalk

organic cinnamon (1 teaspoon) 2 strawberries in the freezer

1 tblsp flax

blueberries, half a cup (frozen or fresh) 3 tbsp. rolled oats (organic)

1 tsp cacao powder

6 oz. almond milk (not sweetened)

In a Nutri Bullet, blitz all of the ingredients until smooth. 8–10 ounces

Calories: 343 | Fat: 12g | Protein: 13g | Carbohydrates: 45g | Sugar: 10g |

Calcium: 13% | Iron: 4.8mg | Vitamin A: 21% | Vitamin C: 41% |

Green Smoothie from Barbara

1 peeled and sliced small orange

2 large spinach handfuls

2 baby bok choi, 1 large kale or chard leaf (nutrition info is for 1 kale leaf)

Frozen mixed berries (half a cup) (nutrition info is for blueberries)

vegan protein powder, 1 serving

10 minutes after soaking 1 teaspoon goji berries

chia seeds, 1 tsp.

1 organic coconut milk, unsweetened

a small amount of water to make the consistency to your liking

Calories: 239 | Fat: 6 g | Protein: 13 g | Carbs: 39 g | Sugar: 21 g | Calcium: 15% | Iron: 3.2 mg | Vitamin A: 91 % | Vitamin C: 219 %

The finished smoothie yields about 4 cups.

I add a small handful of cilantro, a pinch of cayenne pepper, a tablespoon of pureed pumpkin, or a tablespoon of shredded coconut to change things up.

Green Smoothie by Joann

2 quarts spinach

1/2 cup strawberries (tops still attached)

a half cup of blueberries

1 scoop chocolate protein powder (sugar-free)

1 teaspoon cinnamon powder 1 tablespoon flax seed, ground

1/4 cup chia seed, soaked (it will be thick and gelatinous) [approximately 2 tbsp. dry seeds]

a small handful of raw pumpkin seeds or walnuts [nutrition info for 2 tablespoons walnuts is below]

275 calories | 13 g fat | 18 g protein

Carbohydrates: 27g | Sugar: 13g | Calcium: 11%

| Iron: 3.2 milligrams | Vitamin A: 41% | Vitamin C: 89% |

Green Smoothie by Suzanna

a couple of ounces of spinach kale (approximately 2 oz.)

Hemp seeds, 1 ounce

Banana, 136 grams (1 large)

If I want it sweeter, I add a pinch of Stevia.

1.5 to 2 cups water

345 calories | 15 grams of fat | 14 grams of protein | 41 grams of carbohydrates | 17 grams of sugar | 14 percent calcium

| 4.1 mg iron | 79 percent vitamin A | 128 percent vitamin C

Green Smoothie by Chris

8 oz almond milk, unsweetened

2-3 cups spinach (or any other leafy green) I also use kale and arugula.) (This recipe serves 2 cups spinach)

1 peeled medium banana 1 avocado (small)

Calories: 282 | Fat: 13g | Protein: 6g | Carbs: 36g | Sugar: 15g | Calcium: 6% | Iron: 2.4mg | Vitamin A: 41% | Vitamin C: 47% | Calcium: 6% | Iron: 2.4mg

First, combine the milk and greens in a blender. The banana and avocado should be added last because they thicken the smoothie.

Green Smoothie by Sherrikale, 2 cup

cucumber (one)

one celery stalk

2 cups frozen fruit pieces (peaches, nectarines, plums, etc.)

pineapple and mango) (nutrition info is for 2 cups peaches)

1/2 small avocado 1 frozen banana (peeled)

1 lemon (peeled and cut into quarters)

water (16 oz.)

This recipe yields 2 quarts of liquid. Last but not least, add the protein powder and chia seeds.

476 calories | 15 grams of fat | 14 grams of protein | 89 grams of carbohydrates | 47 grams of sugar | 27 grams of calcium | 4.5 grams of iron | 107 grams of vitamin A | 309 grams of vitamin C | Roz's Green Smoothie

Water with an icy chill

a handful of dandelion greens, and a handful of chickweed

3 tiny leaves spinach* Several sprigs of mint and parsley*

2 tablespoons chia seeds Frozen berries with plain yogurt (about 1/2 cup)

Garden-fresh.

To thicken or dilute, add additional yogurt or water, as needed.

Smoothie that is diabetic-friendly

Recipes

Banana-Avo-Plum

1 bok choy head kale (cup)

a pitted red plum

1/4 avocado 1 medium peeled banana

Calories: 258 | Fat: 9 g | Protein: 7 g | Carbs: 46 g | Sugar: 22 g | Calcium: 16% | Iron: 2.2 mg | Vitamin A: 185 % | Vitamin C: 178 %

Strawberry-Banana

2 bok choy heads (baby)

1 large peeled banana

2 c. strawberries, whole avocado (quarter)

Calories: 296 | Fat: 9 g | Protein: 6 g | Carbs: 56 g | Sugar: 31 g | Calcium: 17% | Iron: 2.9 mg | Vitamin A: 270% | Vitamin C: 330%

Smoothie with Pineapple and Strawberry kale, 1 1/2 c.

parsley, 1/2 c.

2 c pineapple, fresh

1 cup berries, whole 1 large peeled banana

Hemp seeds (1 tbsp)

449 calories | 8 grams of fat | 14 grams of protein | 96 grams of carbohydrates
| 54 grams of sugar | 27 percent calcium | 7.2 mg iron | 116 percent vitamin A
| 605 percent vitamin C | Diabetic-Friendly "Green Ice Creams"

Icing Chocolate (makes two servings) coconut milk (1 cup)

cacao powder, 3 teaspoons stevia 7 drops (optional)

avocado (half)

Depending on your ice, roughly 2 cups

In a high-powered blender or food processor, combine all ingredients on medium speed.

286 calories | 22 g fat | 7 g protein | 21 g carbohydrates | 1 g sugar | 11 % calcium | 3.1 mg iron | 22 % vitamin A | 13 % vitamin C | Spinach Ice Cream (makes two servings) Almond milk, 1 cup

stevia 7 drops

spinach, 2 cups

1 tsp vanilla extract ice, 2 cups

In a high-powered blender or food processor, combine all ingredients on medium speed.

Calories: 72 | Fat: 4 g | Protein: 3 g | Carbs: 5 g | Sugar: 1 g | Calcium: 43% | Iron: 2.4mg | Vitamin A: 62% | Vitamin C: 22% | Strawberry Banana Smoothie

Serving Size: 1

Blend on high until everything is well combined in a blender:

1 quart unsweetened almond milk

12 cup plain yogurt, unsweetened (or unsweetened plain kefir)

2 stevia granules (I use Sweet Leaf brand)

1 banana, chopped

1 cup strawberries (fresh or frozen)

1 tsp PaleoFiber powder (or equivalent)

chia seed or flaxseed meal may be substituted)

1 tsp. hydrolyzed collagen (or Vanilla protein powder of your choice)

1 teaspoon extract de vanille

276 calories per serving, 44.7 grams of carbohydrate, 2.6 grams of total fat,

14.3 grams of fiber, and 16.7 grams of protein

(Serves 1) Snickers Smoothie

Blend on high until everything is well combined in a blender:

1 quart unsweetened almond milk

12 cup plain yogurt, unsweetened (or unsweetened plain kefir)

2 stevia granules (I use Sweet Leaf brand)

1 tbsp. cocoa powder (unsweetened)

5 tsp. stevia extract (English Toffee)

1 tbsp. smooth almond butter or peanut butter (no sugar added)

1 tsp PaleoFiber powder (or equivalent)

chia seed or flaxseed meal may be substituted)

1 tsp. hydrolyzed collagen (or Vanilla protein powder of your choice)

1 teaspoon extract de vanille

Greenie is a fictional character.

Smoothie tonic that's both nutritional and tasty.

apple, pear, and kale or spinach

Cinnamon, grapes, fresh mint, and lime juice Healthy, vegan, and kosher are all words that come to mind when thinking about this recipe.

INGREDIENTS

1.5 quarts of water

1 organic ripe green apple, core removed and sliced into bits

1 organic ripe green pear (core removed) cut into bits

2 cups fresh kale or spinach, coarsely chopped

12 cup fresh organic mint, coarsely chopped

12 ice cubes and 20 cold green or moscato grapes

cinnamon, 3/4 tsp

1 teaspoon stevia, 1 tablespoon agave nectar, or more to taste (we use 1

Truvia packet)

lime (one) (juiced, or more to taste) ADDITIONAL REQUIREMENTS a mixing bowl (powerful blender like a Vitamix is best, but any countertop blender will do)

INSTRUCTIONS

Into the blender, pour 12 cups cold water. 1 tblsp. apple and pear chunks Blend until the liquid content of the mixture reaches 100%. Continue to add the apple and pear pieces in tiny handfuls, mixing each one until all of the fruit chunks are incorporated in.

Blend in batches until all of the greens are incorporated in, one handful at a time. Combine the grapes, ice cubes, cinnamon, agave or stevia, and lime juice in a blender and blend until smooth. Blend until the ice has completely broken down.

The cubes have been crushed completely, and the mixture has been smoothed out. To make sure all the greens are completely crushed, I mix it for at least 1 minute.

Serve. My husband and I split this dish into two big cups, even though it serves three medium-sized people. After we've filled our glasses, there's always a little left over, which we normally share. This is the finest health tonic I've ever come across. We feel refreshed, invigorated, and ready to face the day every time we drink it.

Take care to complete the steps in the correct sequence. The components will not mix correctly if you push them all into the blender at the same time.

Carol's Green Smoothie is a refreshing drink that is packed with vitamins and minerals.

1 inch fresh ginger root juice (put it through my Omega Vertical Juicer, then add approximately 1/4 cup water to assist wash out all the juice, and then hand press the pulp to get it all)

8 oz. water, plus more if it's too thick afterward.

1-2 tsp ground cinnamon (I use the Costco cinnamon bottles)

Simply squeeze the bottle for around 2-3 seconds.)

turmeric, 1/4 tsp coconut oil, 1 tbsp chia seeds (1 tblsp)

1 tsp cacao powder, unprocessed

cayenne pepper bottle, 1-2 shakes (to taste)

If desired, 1 tsp kelp powder and 1 tbsp dried goji berries may be added.

Allow the chia seeds and goji berries to soften in the Vitamix before serving.

As you're waiting for the remainder of the frozen ingredients to come out of the freezer:

fresh spouts, 1/2 to 1 cup (I just grab a handful)

1-2 tiny frozen banana pieces (I let my bananas ripen to perfection, then cut them in thirds or quarters depending on their size, place them on a cookie sheet in the freezer until frozen, then transfer to a ziplock bag and store in freezer — never lose bananas due to overripening)

a quarter cup of frozen blueberries (heaping) or

mixture of berries

3 frozen delicious cherries (only for sweetness; fewer or none may be used)

Start on low and gradually increase to high, mixing for approximately a minute. Fill a large cup or tumbler halfway with the mixture.

This isn't very sweet, but it's packed with diabetic-friendly ingredients. Take it for breakfast, then have a green smoothie for lunch or supper, and eat one small meal of ordinary food in between.

If kombucha or another fermented beverage is available, include it.

in place of some of the water, a fermented drink Maintain blood glucose levels in the usual range for fasting and about 120 for eating while making the two smoothies (cacao and green).

One cacao smoothie and one green smoothie (containing spinach, celery, 1 frozen banana, spouts, and perhaps a portion of an avocado) should be had each day.

Strawberry Smoothie with Less Carbohydrates This is the ideal combo for a smoothie that keeps my blood sugar in check while still tasting fantastic!

Course Desserts, beverages, and entrees are all available. Cook Time: 5 minutes Total Time: 5 minutes Low-Carb, Vegetarian Servings 1 glass of juice Per serving, there are 167 calories. Ingredients

5 strawberries of medium size

1 gallon soy milk (unsweetened) (or unsweetened almond milk)

1/2 cup Greek yogurt (low-fat) 6 cubes ice

Instructions

Blend all of the ingredients until smooth in a blender.

Place a strawberry on top and serve in a glass.

Smoothie that is good for diabetics Almond milk, 1 cup

2 c. spinach, washed

protein powder (1-2 scoops) 1 frozen banana

1 tablespoon concentrated frozen apple juice ice cubes (about 6-8 oz.)

This recipe makes two 8-ounce smoothie glasses.

recipe for a smoothie 1 piece of fruit

1 piece of fruit

1 spud

1 stick celery (complete)

1 yuzu

1 skinned lemon

cinnamon powder (1 teaspoon) cayenne pepper (1/2 teaspoon) 1 c. ice-cold water

This recipe provides enough food for three days.

Diabetic Oatmeal Breakfast Breakfast Smoothie with Oats Smoothie is a quick and substantial morning beverage that is a terrific way to start the day! Breakfast is served.

American cuisine.

Breakfast smoothie made with oats 2 people

dieTTaste is an author. Ingredients

1 cup uncooked oats, ground in a spice or coffee grinder, or processed in a food processor

first 3 cup skim milk 2 frozen bananas, sliced into tiny bits

2 tsp sugar replacement (ground flaxseed)

2 tblsp coffee (instant) (optional) Instructions

Blend all of the ingredients in a blender, immersion blender, or food processor until smooth.

In a glass, pour the Oatmeal Breakfast Smoothie.

CPSIA information can be obtained
at www.ICGtesting.com
Printed in the USA
LVHW061659240122
709145LV00009B/626

9 781804 371527